IMPORTANT

HERE IS YOUR REGISTRATION CODE TO ACCESS MCGRAW-HILL PREMIUM CONTENT AND MCGRAW-HILL ONLINE RESOURCES

For key premium online resources you need THIS CODE to gain access. Once the code is entered, you will be able to use the web resources for the length of your course.

Access is provided only if you have purchased a new book.

If the registration code is missing from this book, the registration screen on our website, and within your WebCT or Blackboard course will tell you how to obtain your new code. Your registration code can be used only once to establish access. It is not transferable.

To gain access to these online resources

1. USE your web browser to go to: **www.mhhe.com/lenkeit3**

2. CLICK on "First Time User"

3. ENTER the Registration Code printed on the tear-off bookmark on the right

4. After you have entered your registration code, click on "Register"

5. FOLLOW the instructions to setup your personal UserID and Password

6. WRITE your UserID and Password down for future reference. Keep it in a safe place.

If your course is using WebCT or Blackboard, you'll be able to use this code to access the McGraw-Hill content within your instructor's online course.

To gain access to the McGraw-Hill content in your instructor's WebCT or Blackboard course simply log into the course with the user ID and Password provided by your instructor. Enter the registration code exactly as it appears to the right when prompted by the system. You will only need to use this code the first time you click on McGraw-Hill content.

These instructions are specifically for student access. Instructors are not required to register via the above instructions.

The McGraw-Hill Companies

 Higher Education

Thank you, and welcome to your McGraw-Hill Online Resources.

ISBN-13: 978-0-07-310776-9
ISBN-10: 0-07-310776-X
T/A LENKEIT: INTRODUCING CULTURAL ANTHROPOLOGY, 3/E

INTRODUCING
CULTURAL
ANTHROPOLOGY

CURRENT WORLD POLITICAL REGIONS

ABBREVIATIONS

ALB.	ALBANIA
AUST.	AUSTRIA
BELG.	BELGIUM
BOS.	BOSNIA AND HERZEGOVINA
BULG.	BULGARIA
DEN.	DENMARK
DOM. REP.	DOMINICAN REPUBLIC
CRO.	CROATIA
CZECH.	CZECH REPUBLIC
EST.	ESTONIA
GER.	GERMANY
HUNG.	HUNGARY
LAT.	LATVIA
LITH.	LITHUANIA
LUX.	LUXEMBURG
MAC.	MACEDONIA
NETH.	NETHERLANDS
ROM.	ROMANIA
RUSS.	RUSSIA
SER.	SERBIA and MONTENEGRO
SLOVK.	SLOVAKIA
SLOVN.	SLOVENIA
SWITZ.	SWITZERLAND
U.A.E.	UNITED ARAB EMIRATES

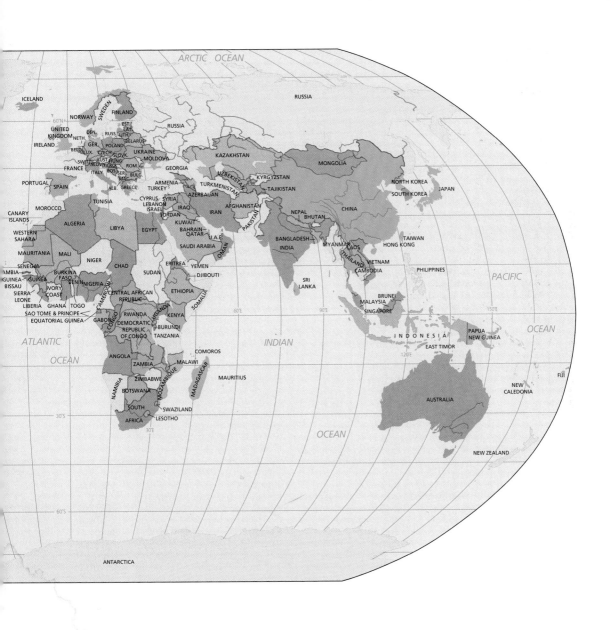

INTRODUCING CULTURAL ANTHROPOLOGY

Third Edition

Roberta Edwards Lenkeit
Modesto Junior College

Boston   Burr Ridge, IL   Dubuque, IA   Madison, WI   New York
San Francisco   St. Louis   Bangkok   Bogotá   Caracas   Kuala Lumpur
Lisbon   London   Madrid   Mexico City   Milan   Montreal   New Delhi
Santiago   Seoul   Singapore   Sydney   Taipei   Toronto

Higher Education

Published by McGraw-Hill, an imprint of The McGraw-Hill Companies, Inc. 1221 Avenue of the Americas, New York, NY 10020. Copyright © 2007, by the McGraw-Hill Companies, Inc. All rights reserved. Previous edition © 2001 by Mayfield Publishing Company. No part of this publication may be reproduced or distributed in any form or by any means, or stored in a database or retrieval system, without the prior written permission of The McGraw-Hill Companies, Inc., including but not limited to, in any network or other electronic storage or transmission, or broadcast for distance learning. Some ancillaries, including electronic and print components, may not be available to customers outside the United States.

This book is printed on acid-free paper.

1 2 3 4 5 6 7 8 9 0 VNH / VNH 0 9 8 7 6

ISBN-13: 978-0-07-310773-8
ISBN-10: 0-07-310773-5

Publisher: *Phillip A. Butcher*
Sponsoring editor: *Kevin Witt*
Development editor: *Thom Holmes*
Marketing manager: *Dan Loch*
Production editor: *Anne Fuzellier*
Production supervisor: *Rich DeVitto*
Design manager: *Cassandra Chu*
Cover design: *William Stanton*
Interior design: *Linda Roberston and Glenda King*
Art editor: *Robin Mouat*
Manager, photo research: *Brian Pecko*
PowerPoints: *Mark Stephens*
Compositor: *Thompson Type*
Text and paper: *Printed in 10/12 Janson on 50# Publishers Matte*
Printer: *Von Hoffman Press*
Cover image: Eagle Hunters of Mongolia, © Hamid Sardar/Corbis

Library of Congress Cataloging In-Publication Data

Lenkeit, Roberta Edwards.
    Introducing cultural anthropology / Roberta Edwards Lenkeit.—3rd ed.
      p. cm.
    Includes bibliographical references and index.
    ISBN-13: 978-0-07-310773-8 (alk. paper)
    ISBN-10: 0-07-310773-5 (alk. paper)
      1. Ethnology. I. Title.

GN316.L46 2006
306—dc22
                                     2006040988

www.mhhe.com

To Don and Allison
for all of the 3PRIM8 memories

BRIEF CONTENTS

�֎ CONTENTS

4 Language: Is This What Makes Us Human?   72

PART TWO
CROSS-CULTURAL ADAPTIVE PATTERNS   93

5 Subsistence Strategies and Resource Allocation I: What Challenges Face Foragers?   94

ANTHROPOLOGY AROUND US BOXES

TO THE INSTRUCTOR

THE STORY OF THE BOOK

I decided to write this text when driving across the country during a sabbatical leave. My husband (also an anthropologist) and I were discussing the selection of a text for the following semester — again. This quest repeated itself every year. Our approaches and styles of teaching the introductory cultural anthropology course are different, but we share common goals: to assure that students learn the basic concepts and approaches of anthropology; to focus on the usefulness of the anthropological approach to their lives; to introduce the field and its holistic nature; and to highlight the scientific nature of anthropology. We have each used nearly every text on the market at one time. And we were frustrated. We were frustrated by encyclopedic texts, by texts that emphasized theory and were written in styles that were too formal, by shorter texts that lacked visual interest and targeted upper division students, and by texts that seemed to ignore the other fields of anthropology. We discovered that many colleagues shared our frustration.

At the time I belonged to (and still do) a unique, semiformal group of anthropologists in northern California who taught introductory level anthropology courses at different types of colleges, both two and four year. The focus of our get-togethers was pedagogy. We shared what works. Listening to concerns of colleagues in this forum contributed to my desire to write a text that was relatively short, more informal, and built around pedagogy that incorporated the holistic nature of anthropology and emphasized the scientific approach.

THE APPROACH OF THE TEXT

The last twenty-five years have seen a dramatic increase in both the data of anthropology and in theoretical issues within the discipline. It is impossible to fit everything into an introductory course, and it is my view that it is also pedagogically unsound. Less can be more. I have come to the conclusion, based on teaching introductory anthropology courses for more than thirty years, that my main task as a teacher is to excite students about the *possibilities* of anthropology and to teach them the core perspectives, concepts, and methods of anthropology.

I have also endeavored to write an approachable text. I tried to write as though I am talking directly to the student while maintaining an appropriate scholarly tone. In many places throughout the text, I have included examples and stories to which students can relate so that they can see how anthropology is part of our everyday lives.

Pedagogy has also been an important part of my overall design. As I wrote, I kept in mind the importance of signposting important concepts and presenting a reasonable number of detailed examples to illustrate points. Concepts are also presented visually wherever possible. Students are asked to apply concepts they have learned throughout the book.

Ideas are also reinforced throughout the text — the holistic, comparative, scientific, and humanistic perspectives of the discipline. The occasional relevant issue from archaeology and biological anthropology is woven into the text to emphasize the holistic view. Students are asked in the Try This feature to make hypotheses and devise ways to test them. Contributions of the humanistic perspective are also noted.

The text is designed as an anchor text so that ethnographies, topical books, and collections of readings can be part of the course's assigned readings. I believe that including such books gives students in-depth insights into one culture and a holistic perspective on topics. I believe strongly that students need an anchor text that presents basic concepts in the field and provides a framework around which the ethnographies, other readings, and lectures can build.

I've used an eclectic approach to theoretical issues throughout, and I've used ones that are practical as part of my "less-is-more" philosophy and pedagogical approach. When students have a firm understanding of a few paradigms, they have a foundation on which to examine others — and think critically about all.

◎ HALLMARK FEATURES

- A manageable number of brief chapters, which can easily be covered in a semester, offer a brief introduction to the field.
- An emphasis throughout on how anthropology is relevant to students can be found in many examples and stories. In addition, the final two chapters demonstrate the relevance of anthropology to students' future lives — in their work and in their community.

- A pedagogy that asks students to think critically. The Try This activity prompts are integrated throughout the text and ask students to ponder, compare, analyze, hypothesize, and apply the concepts they have just read about. These are purposefully written at a variety of levels. A few are simple and don't require much analytical thought (for example, those labeled Ponder or Consider). Others require more engagement by asking students to discuss issues. Those with prompts such as Compare, Contrast, Analyze, Apply, and Hypothesize are intended to stimulate students' integrative thought process by helping them apply concepts, perspectives, and methods.

- Learning objectives, chapter summaries, study questions, and suggested readings at the end of chapters offer learning support.

- A strong visual appeal achieved through a wealth of concept illustrations and color photos. This provides pedagogical support for students.

- Two chapters unique to briefer texts: a chapter on fieldwork that offers firsthand accounts of the challenges of acquiring data, and a chapter that looks at sexuality across cultures. Both of these are topics that beginning students are curious about, and both topics stimulate lively debate.

- Organization by standard topics to fit the teaching styles of most professors, while at the same time reflecting my pedagogical focus for students by clustering chapters into three sections: basic concepts and methods, cross-cultural adaptive patterns, and applying the anthropological perspective.

- A personal writing style applauded by reviewers.

◎ WHAT'S NEW TO THIS EDITION

- New section in Chapter 13 on **Anthropology and Globalization** includes material on **colonialism** and **hegemony** with focus on **tourism** studies and **ethical dilemmas,** plus technology and mass communication. Another new section **Culture Change: A Brief Historical Overview** has material on theory. Substantially revised sections include How Cultures Change and How Change Is Studied.

- New Chapters 5 and 6 expand previous coverage of subsistence strategies and resource allocations, as follow:

    - Chapter 5, **Subsistence Strategies and Resource Allocation I: What Challenges Face Foragers,** contains more background on models of cultural evolution and cultural ecology and updates on foragers today.

- Chapter 6, **Subsistence Strategies and Resource Allocation II: How Did Food Production Transform Culture?,** contains expanded material on agriculture and features associated with intensive agricultural lifeways, including more material on stratification in chiefdoms and states, and new materials on market exchange and currency use.

- **New and Updated Anthropology Around Us boxes.** These boxes focus on current and timely issues that illustrate how the perspectives, topics, and concepts of anthropology are part of our everyday lives. Changes include
  - Chapter 6, "Is Slow Food Making a Fast Comeback?"
  - Chapter 9, "Does Gender Affect Attitudes About Circumcision?"
  - Substantial update of Chapter 7 box, "Outdated Traditions?"
  - Other **boxes are updated throughout.**

- Expanded **glossary** and expanded **marginal running glossary** help students to focus on important terms as they are introduced.

- Several new and updated **chapter openers** provide vignettes that relate to the chapter's contents. Well received in the book's second edition, these are designed to draw the student into the chapter and show the relevance of the topics to their lives.

- Chapter 3, **Fieldwork,** includes new ethnographic-based material on life shock.

- Chapter 7, **Marriage, Family, and Residence,** has an expanded section on sister exchange marriage and an expanded Anthropology Around Us box that includes marriage finance.

- Chapter 8, **Kinship and Descent,** is updated with a revised section on kindred groups within bilateral descent systems and a new section on **Voluntary Association Groups.**

- Chapter 10, **Political Order, Disorder, and Social Control,** includes more text discussion on homicide in foraging societies and updated statistics in Table 10.1 on **Murder Rates.**

◎ SUPPLEMENTS

As a full-service publisher of quality educational products, McGraw-Hill does much more than just sell textbooks. They create and publish an extensive array of print, video, and digital supplements for students and instructors. *Introducing Cultural Anthropology* boasts a comprehensive supplement package. Orders of new (versus used) textbooks help to defray the cost of developing such supplements, which is substantial. Please consult your local McGraw-Hill representative for more information on any of the supplements.

For the Student

The Student's Online Learning Center   This free, Web-based, partially password protected, student supplement features a large number of helpful tools, activities, links, and useful information at *www.mhhe.com/lenkeit3*. To access the password-protected areas of the site, students must purchase a new copy of the text. Designed specifically to complement the individual chapters of the text, students access material by text chapter. Exciting activities and resources include

- Try This Internet exercises that offer chapter-related links to Web sites and activities for students to complete based on those sites.
- Chapter objectives, outlines, and overviews that are designed to give students signposts for understanding and recognizing key chapter content.
- PowerPoint lecture notes that offer point-by-point notes of chapter sections.
- Multiple choice and true/false questions that give students the opportunity to quiz themselves on chapter content.
- Essay questions that allow students to explore key chapter concepts through their own writing.
- A glossary that illustrates key terms.
- An audio glossary that helps students with difficult-to-pronounce words through audio pronunciation help.
- Vocabulary flashcards that allow students to test their mastery of key vocabulary terms.
- General Web links that offer chapter-by-chapter links for further research.
- Links to *New York Times* articles where students have immediate access to articles on chapter-related content.
- Links to useful information on careers in anthropology.

PowerWeb   This feature is offered free with the purchase of a new copy of the text and is available via a link on the Student's Online Learning Center. PowerWeb helps students with online research by providing access to high-quality academic sources. PowerWeb is a password-protected site that provides students with the full text of course-specific, peer-reviewed articles from the scholarly and popular press, as well as Web links, student study tools, weekly updates, and additional resources. For further information about PowerWeb, visit *www.dushkin.com/powerweb/pwwt1.mhtml*.

For the Instructor

The Instructor's Resource CD-ROM   This easy-to-use disk provides

- PowerPoint lecture slides that give professors ready-made chapter-by-chapter presentation notes.
- A computerized test bank offering numerous multiple choice, short answer, and essay questions in an easy-to-use program. McGraw-Hill's EZ Test is a flexible and easy-to-use electronic testing program. The program allows instructors to create tests from book-specific items. It accommodates a wide range of question types, and instructors may add their own questions. Multiple versions of the test can be created, and any test can be exported for use with course management systems such as WebCT, BlackBoard or PageOut. EZ Test Online is a new service and gives you a place to easily administer your EZ Test-created exams and quizzes online. The program is available for Windows and Macintosh environments.
- A complete Instructor's Manual offering helpful teaching tips along with chapter-by-chapter overviews, learning objectives, outlines, key terms, and suggested class activities.

The Instructor's Online Learning Center   This password-protected site offers access to all of the student online materials plus important instructor support materials and downloadable supplements such as

- An image library that offers professors the opportunity to create custom-made, professional looking presentations and handouts by providing electronic versions of many of the maps, charts, line art, and photos in the text along with additional relevant images not included in the text. All images are ready to be used in any applicable teaching tools including the professor's own lecture materials or McGraw-Hill provided PowerPoint lecture slides.
- A complete Instructor's Manual offers helpful teaching tips along with chapter-by-chapter overviews, learning objectives, outlines, key terms, and suggested class activities.
- PowerPoint lecture slides give professors ready made chapter-by-chapter presentation notes.
- Links to professional resources provide useful links to professional anthropological sites on the Internet.

PowerWeb   This resource is available via a link on the Instructor's Online Learning Center. PowerWeb helps with online research by providing access to high-quality academic sources. PowerWeb is a password-protected site that provides instructors with the full text of course-specific, peer-reviewed articles from the scholarly and popular press, as well as Web links, weekly updates, and additional resources. For further information about PowerWeb, visit *www.dushkin.com/powerweb/pwwt1.mhtml.*

PageOut: The Course Web Site Development Center   All online content for the text is supported by WebCT, Blackboard, eCollege.com, and other course management systems. Additionally, McGraw-Hill's PageOut service is available to get professors and their courses up and running online in a matter of hours, at no cost. PageOut was designed for instructors just beginning to explore Web options. Even a novice computer user can create a course Web Site with a template provided by McGraw-Hill (no programming knowledge necessary). To learn more about PageOut, visit *www.mhhe.com/pageout.*

Videotapes   A wide variety of full-length videotapes from the *Films for the Humanities and Sciences* series is available to adopters of the text.

◉ ACKNOWLEDGMENTS

Special acknowledgment, love, and gratitude to my husband, best friend, and colleague, Don A. Lenkeit. In this, as in previous editions, his eagle eye, in-house editing, and generous gift of assistance (plus an uncanny ability to provide sustenance just when I needed it on those long writing days) kept the project going. He also again co-authored the Instructor's Manual and Online Learning Center. Thanks to our daughter and colleague K. Allison Lenkeit Meezan. She even took time from tending baby Katherine to read sections and make suggestions. To the resident felines — Mr. Darwin for monitoring the printer, and Mrs. Hobbes for paperweight duty — your attentiveness to this edition was appreciated.

I am grateful to colleague and friend Debra Bolter for being an astute sounding board for revision ideas and for reading and commenting on various sections. To Bill Fairbanks for your many insightful suggestions, thank you. To Rob Edwards and the members of the California Community College Anthropology Teacher's group (formerly the A 2-4-6 group), thanks for all of the years of stimulating meetings on the teaching of anthropology. To Jan Beatty who supported this project in the first place, you will always be a part of it, as will all of the wonderful folks at Mayfield. The reviewers of previous editions whose suggestions are reflected here still, I acknowledge and thank you again.

Special appreciation to Kevin Witt, senior editor Anthropology/ Criminal Justice, who continues to believe in this project, and to senior development editor Thom Holmes for his guidance with this edition. I am indebted to Brian Pecko, photo research manager, who is a pleasure to work with and excels at locating the perfect image. Thanks also to editorial coordinator Teresa Treacy, for attending to myriad details; production editor Anne Fuzellier, for making the process go smoothly; design manager Cassandra Chu and art editor Robin Mouat, for the appealing design and visuals; copyeditor Joan Pendleton, for her eagle eye; sales manager Dan Loch and his team, for all of their marketing acumen; and production supervisor Randy Hurst, for bringing the various pieces together.

The reviewers of this edition are owed my special thanks for all of their insightful comments and many helpful suggestions. They are

Marc A. Rees, University of Louisiana at Lafayette

Lynne Miller, Mira Costa College

Katherine C. Donohue, Plymouth State University

Art Barbeau, West Liberty State College

Christina Beard-Moose, Suffolk County Community College

Jon A. Schlenker, University of Maine at Augusta

Mary Kay Gilliland, Pima Community College

Margaret S. Bruchez, Blinn College

Carl Hefner, University of Hawaii–Kapiolani Community College

Jennifer Molina-Stidger, Sierra College

Amy J. Hirshman, University of Michigan–Flint

Shepherd M. Jenks Jr., Albuquerque TVI Community College

TO THE STUDENT

Anthropology often conjures up exotic visions of distant peoples, places, and customs. But this is only part of what cultural anthropology is about. It is about examining humanity from every angle and looking at how all aspects interrelate — what we call the holistic approach. It is about the common denominators of the human experience, as well as the differences. What constitutes the exotic is usually no more than those customs different from our own. I've written this text as a brief introduction to the core concepts in cultural anthropology. It is a summary of what we have learned from our quest to understand the adaptive patterns of human cultures.

My philosophy of teaching is that less can be more. If you can digest a concept and a solid example, I believe that you will remember it. Too many examples when you are first learning about a subject can muddy everything. If you engage with this text, you will have a strong foundation to do further work in anthropology. Even if you don't plan to go on in anthropology, the perspectives of anthropology will provide you with much that is useful. Cultural anthropology is applicable to many fields — health care, law enforcement, education, retail business, and any other field that requires working with people. Anthropology is inherently fascinating. We discover things about ourselves as we examine other cultures, and I hope that you will enjoy this process of discovery.

HOW TO USE THIS BOOK

You'll find many learning tools both within the text and at the text's Online Learning Center:

- Objectives at the beginning of each chapter state the aims of the chapter and are signposts to what you will learn. If you carefully read these and the chapter summary first, you will have an excellent framework to help you focus as you read. Additionally, chapter objectives, chapter outlines, chapter overviews, and PowerPoint lecture notes are available at the Student's Online Learning Center. This free Web-based, partially password-protected, supplement can be found at *www.mhhe.com/lenkeit3*.

- Important anthropological concepts and terms are set in bold type throughout the text and are clearly explained. The running glossary placed in the margins helps you to focus on these important terms, and the glossary at the back of the book provides an alphabetical list of all these terms along with their definitions. Go to the Online Learning Center to test your mastery of key vocabulary by using the vocabulary flashcards. The audio glossary at this site helps you with difficult-to-pronounce words.

- Study questions appear at the end of each chapter so that you can test yourself on chapter content. Multiple choice and true/false questions posted at the Online Learning Center give you the opportunity to quiz yourself on chapter content and receive immediate feedback. Essay questions allow you to explore key chapter concepts through your own writing.

- The Try This prompts in the text were written to actively engage you with the material you've just read. Some of them are rather simple, and you can respond by just thinking about them. Others require you to be analytical and ask you to demonstrate your creativity and critical thinking skills. Recent research in the field of cognitive science reinforces that learning is tied to active involvement with a subject. Bottom line — if you engage with the Try This exercises, you will learn more about anthropology. Additionally, Try This Internet exercises at the Online Learning Center offer chapter-related links to Web sites and activities for you to complete based on these sites.

- References within the text are placed in parentheses and the full reference can be found in the bibliography. You'll also find suggested readings that will direct you to sources for further study. The Web site addresses I've provided were current at the time the book went to press.

- More activities and links are available at the Online Learning Center, such as additional Web links, links to *New York Times* related articles, and links to information on careers in anthropology, plus PowerWeb — an online research tool that provides you access to full text articles from high-quality academic sources and more.

◎ NEW TO THIS EDITION

The text has been **updated throughout.** There are now **two new chapters** on subsistence strategies and resource allocation — one focuses on foraging societies and the other on societies that produce food. This provides chapters of more manageable length. The important topic of globalization is now included with examples drawn from tourism and mass media.

❀ WALKTHROUGH

A Brief Text ▶

With its manageable number of brief chapters, *Introducing Cultural Anthropology* offers a concise introduction to the field, which can easily be covered in a semester and be supplemented by ethnographies, topical books, and collections of readings.

◀ Unique Applications

Students are asked to think critically and apply concepts they have learned throughout the book in unique Try This activities.

A Lively Writing Style ▶

Spiced with humor, anecdotes, and an overall conversational tone, *Introducing Cultural Anthropology* reflects the author's thirty years of award-winning teaching and her understanding of how to reach beginning students.

◄ Anthropology Around Us

This stimulating boxed feature focuses on current and timely issues that illustrate how the perspectives, topics, and concepts of anthropology are part of our everyday lives.

Enticing Chapter Openers ►

New and updated chapter openers provide vignettes that are designed to draw the student into the chapter content and show how anthropology is relevant.

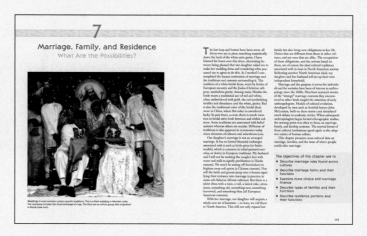

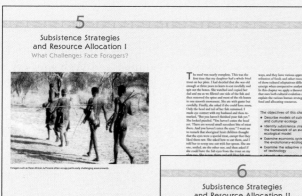

◄ Two New Chapters Expand Coverage

Two chapters on subsistence and resource allocation provide more coverage than the previous one chapter in the last edition.

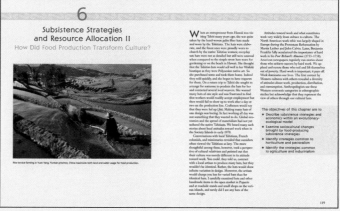

An Outstanding Visual Program ▶

A strong visual appeal, achieved through a wealth of unique concept illustrations and color photos, provides pedagogical support for students.

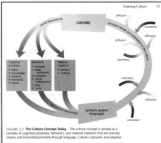

◀ Extensive Supporting Pedagogy

Learning objectives, chapter summaries, study questions, suggested readings, and Web sites offer learning support in every chapter.

Helpful Marginal Support ▶

The marginal thumbnail maps highlight the appropriate area under discussion while a new marginal running glossary helps students focus on terms as they are introduced.

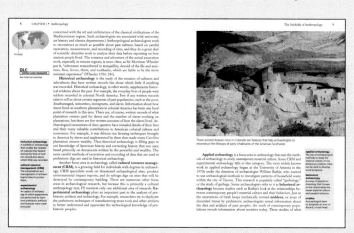

◀ Help on Reading Ethnographies

The appendix "How Do You Read an Ethnography?" gives students practical steps that they can take to get the most out of reading ethnographies and comparing ethnographies to one another.

Updated Online Learning Center Web Site ▶

This free Web-based supplement offers students a large number of helpful tools, activities, links, and useful information while offering professors an Image Bank and other valuable resources. In-text icons clearly guide students to information on a particular topic that is available on the Online Learning Center.